Under A Guiding Star

A Poetic Adventure

Gordon Draper

Printed in the United States of America

ISBN: 9798836096328

10 9 8 7 6 5 4 3 2 1

EMPIRE PUBLISHING
www.empirebookpublishing.com

For
Philip, Linda I., D. Charmaine Patricia A.

Table of Contents

INTRODUCTION

The Guiding Star

Navigation is an acquired skill that we need to get us to our chosen destination, or a given point, place, or area of interest.

In order to find our way, we need the help of a good memory, a G.P.S., Compass, Sextant, or knowledge of the stars above, for the geographical area in which we are located at a given point in time.

For those of us in the Northern Hemisphere, and particularly for sailors on the North Atlantic Ocean we would look for and locate a star we often call The North Star, or Polaris, and calculate their position and direction based upon that star.

Polaris appears in the night sky almost directly above Earth's rotational axis.

Unlike other stars which appear like they are spinning around the axis, as the earth turns; Polaris seems to stay in place.

So, by setting a course based on our position as it relates to this star, we will be heading due north, if we are in the Northern Hemisphere.

Polaris is in the Constellation called Ursa, and is one of the stars in the Little Dipper group. Polaris is one of the more important stars of recent times.

Now, above the heavenly stars is another heaven, and yet again, another heaven, a third heaven. This is the place where a Christian Believer's Guiding Star resides.

This Spiritual Star I am talking about here is called Jesus and he reigns there in heaven, at God's right hand.

Jesus Christ was there in the beginning, sent to Earth as a newborn Babe, and was crucified. died and was resurrected, rose again, to ascend back to heaven where he awaits his second return to earth to gather up his Church...those Christian Believers...who are still on earth at that time.

This Jesus Christ is our Guiding Star, and for believers, He is the way, the truth, and the Light, and guide to our final heavenly destination and eternal life.

When we experience the passing of a loved one from this earthly life to another eternal life in heaven, it is important to spend time defining in our minds, the nature of that individual.

Being the Parents of the one who has gone on to their reward ahead of us, it is important to share with the remaining family group what we believe defined Pamela as a Daughter, Wife, Sister, and Aunt. It is important to know, that Pam truly loved all of her family members.

There are five Character traits that best apply to Pamela, in my mind, and they are Love, Loyalty, Courage, Leadership, and Creativity.

Her love was Outgoing Love, she gave more, and received much from family in return.

Loyalty was so important to Pam. She never threw anyone "under the bus." She accepted the slings and arrows from others, she hurt for a while but bounced back to listen to the concerns of others. She never gave up on any one of us, regardless of the circumstances.

Of all her outstanding traits I would list Courage as the single, most dominant factor.

Pam's courage is most visible when you consider the never-give-up mindset, she exhibited in dealing with her long, debilitating physical setbacks for some twenty-five years. She always thought in terms of getting better, and she would identify needs and followed-up with solutions.

Her Leadership quality was such that she always led a group in the work-a-day world by offering the best way forward, but never taking credit, but pointed to others as the reasons for success. She created a positive environment.

Pam's thinking was clear and accurate which was at the root of her creativity. She was able to define a challenge quickly, make a decision, and create the needed solution that was right on target.

On many days we would talk on the 'phone for about an hour. These talks would begin with the status of her condition, her concerns, and her frustrations. Then she quickly turned to talk about her current project.

During her last venture, it was being a guest on a Radio Political Talk program where she would offer her take on current political events. To prepare for each call-in, she would review various reports and print media offerings as well as TV political News.

Such are the things that occupied her days, in order to distract from the daily battle with pain, anguish, and worry with financial concerns of the high cost of cancer treatments, until, finally, the body gave out and the Lord God Almighty called her home to her reward.

The preamble and settings I have selected are representative of the challenges or, environment in which most people live. The Poems, I hope, will allow you to move away from the ho-hum, and be transported to a place to think of the wonders that are there for us to seek and enjoy.

The four seasonal settings that follow represent the stepping stones from one phase of our lives to the next, and the journey through our earthly pursuits. Also, the setting of the wilderness is challenging for any journey we face.

My hope is you will find time to ponder when the things of earth grow strangely dim.

Pamela

When dreams, like a soft breeze
Flow through our minds and
Visions of Pamela appear just in time,
For us to enjoy her presence again.
As the peace, of His soothing call, came her way.
And, when a calm fills her soul with grace to move on
to a better resting place. We can smile and know.
All is well with her soul.
God had noticed her helpless estate,
and sounded the trumpet of victory,
While choirs of angels rejoice at her appearing,
and sing of her new life's eternal beginning.
Only weep for our child, your sister, awhile
but dwell on the time when we see her anew.
And celebrate by singing, glory to God in the highest.
For all to see that once again life has won.

Over the Waves

When dreams came in shadows to haunt her nights;
When despair crashes as waves on the deck.
She shouted one more cry: why, why, why!
And her roar echoed back... over the waves.

When memories like a tempest, raced through her mind.
When all hope seemed dashed on the rocks.
She sailed down the night to ride out the storm,
As the wind billows the sails and she flies ...over the waves.

When a voice in a whisper, touched her soul.
When her heart became calm and serene.
There came a new dawn, with His light for her way.
And her spirit soared and flowed...over the waves.

Then a breeze like a fair wind filled her sails,
And the balance of life seemed worth living again.
She set a new course, for a harbor called grace.
It was not too far away.... just over the waves.

Star is in The Sky

Free from this world's grasp.
A flickering light pauses in flight.
Her guardian Angel extends a hand.
And, a celestial odyssey began.
On her way from earth to Heaven.
Cool cleaning waves wash over her.
She is instantly transformed, perfect, and whole.
Her robes of white flow like a comet's trail.
Across the abyss, and growing brighter still,
She soars and sparkles in the deep,
And greets the dawn of her tomorrow with a cheer;
"The best is yet be."
Portals of Pearls, Music majestic and everlasting light,
Guide her way along paths of precious stones,
To a mansion in the City of Gold.
All is in perfect harmony.
Now she stands before His Throne
To receive the Victors Crown.
And The Voice through the Heavens resounds.
"Welcome Home, Welcome Home."

Promises and Principals:

Learning of God's Promises, and developing the Principals for a Personal Constitution are more easily developed when we take advantage of the instructions, for living a Godly life, found in his Word, the Holy Bible.

Also, by searching God's Word, in a deeper way, we are better able to effectively share the truths found therein with others. God's Word is our guide for today and our hope for tomorrow and is so important in the personal way forward for the rest of your life.

As we spend time in The Word we learn that Believers are the recipients of God's Promises, and in the text for each of the "Seasons" that follow you will find Promises and Principals that only apply to Believers, and that only Believers may claim.

When you follow up on God's wish that we read and study His Word, you will discover many more truths to live by each day.

A Spring Day for Renewal

Spring sallies forth reluctantly.

Heavy waves crash on the rocky coast.

As I gaze at distant ships far out to sea.

Winter's grip and Spring's thaw

I wish they didn't last so long.

Yuk, yuk, yuk, yuk.

The Wilderness

Now folks, as you flip the pages of this offering you will enter a time of zero gravity...it's a special time to clear away the debris of the day from your mind and focus on the things that really count in living a winning life.

So, just settle back comfortably...let yourself relax...allow the things of the day to just slip away.

When you are at ease, eject all those whims and goals, all your worries and cares from your thoughts. Next, tap into those dreams and desires that are real possibilities, and perhaps, you will aspire to the life God has in store for you.

This adventure begins atop Maine's rugged peaks, which are strewn with giant boulders and the ever-present blustery winds that change from cool to frigid, depending on the time of year. Relief from these elements will come later when we work our way down to the valley below and arrive at a sturdy cabin just below the soaring peaks in this vast sanctuary near the rock-bound coast of the Atlantic Ocean.

About now you will need to adjust your mindset to be determined, as the adventure ahead unfolds you will find yourself confronted with an enemy who has taken over so many things we hold dear. Also, you may be faced with some choices, like...good over evil, right over wrong, freedom, or enslavement to evil powers.

Depending on where your commitment rests, you might be challenged to exceed yourself.

A Peaceful Easy Feeling

The sky over Mount Katahdin is clear and it has a certain quality in its light that sharpens the lines of the mountain peaks to the north and the rolling landscape to the south, where they meet the sky.

Deep in the heart of Maine is this wilderness called Baxter State Park and it is so preserved that you feel you have found that perfect hiding place away from the tumult caused by a maddening crowd that tends to muddle one's thinking.

Mount Katahdin, in this wilderness, is the northern beginning point of the much trodden Appalachian Trail.

Up here, however, for some trekkers, it is a spooky place where Indian folklore offers tales of strange spirits lurking in notches and caves to do you harm.

According to legend, there is the wandering spirit of Katahdin named "Pamola" which is in a great cavern hereabouts.

Then there is "Gluskap", or the Liar. Gluskap is credited by Indian Lore for creating many of the giant beasts of Katahdin, after which he decided to downsize these enormous beasts, which included a huge moose and beaver; but he had to chase down both the moose and the beaver far and wide.

The tale concludes with the beaver escaping his grasp to the building of Niagara Falls.

The fate of the huge Moose has been lost as earlier generations claim its demise is too horrific to tell.

Winding upward along the trail you come to a place called "Knife Edge". It's a mile-long ridge of rock, only a few feet wide in spots, and it connects Baxter Peak and Pamola Peak.

As I stand here surveying the scene before and below me Knife Edge seems suspended over the abyss between the two peaks. Before embarking on this portion of the trail it's wise to be on the safe side and not attempt a climb during a time of driving, very high, winds that present themselves regularly, so I have tied a set of tell-tails to my hiking stick and raise it high overhead, to get a better understanding of the direction and strength of the winds up here today.

Knife Edge is an acrophobic nightmare, as it is 3,000 feet down to the valley below at one end and it is 4,000 feet down at the other end. If you happen to fall while navigating the edge you won't fall straight down, but you may bounce a few times on your way to the bottom.

There are 45 peaks here that exceed 3,000 feet in elevation, Mount Katahdin is the tallest at close to 5,300 feet, and it appears untouched and unchanged since the beginning of time. All around me are large granite boulders that seem to have been cast aside as rejects by some giant, supernatural stonemason.

My senses, like my awareness and my consciousness, are heightened in this place and intuitively I take stock of things close at hand. The solitary nature of this place rejuvenates those senses of self-preservation that I thought had vanished, because of the softer life we now have in this society.

In this remote place things seem never to change, they are the same today, tomorrow and to the end of time. Now, as I allow these feelings to seep in, I feel a kinship to an earlier time when things were simpler and when dealing with life was a matter of choices we make; and not extraneous influences. So, time and timing, along with choices, in dealing with day-to-day events are important. But, you know, God's timing is impeccable and always precise, isn't it? He is never late. No emergency takes Him by surprise, or beyond His abilities to handle things. After

all, our future is God's past so He knows what's around the corner before we do.

Someone once conjured these word pictures of God at work during the six days of creation, so picture this in your mind's eye: "Standing on nothing, He reached out where there was nowhere to reach and caught something, when there was nothing to catch, and hung something on nothing, and told it to stay there…Standing on nothing he took the hammer of His own will, and He struck the anvil of His omnipotence and sparks flew, and He caught them on the tips of His fingers and flung them out into space and bedecked the heavens with stars!"

Think of God's six days of creation and realize just how spectacular it must have been!

So, I wonder, are we any-the-less spectacular, when we turn our lives over to God, and in response, He installs the Holy Spirit in our deepest being?

Up here, closer to heaven, it is easy to imagine those moments of creation, as in this darkness the earth seems without form; and then as the dawn comes up like a bolt out of the blue, as though God had just said…let there be light!

Sitting here now as the glow from the campfire dims and as the sun slowly rises and transforms the images that surround me. The light seems to have acted as an alarm clock that awakens the sleeping creatures of this place. With the morning light animals move down the mountainside, to a lower elevation and their watering hole at Sandy Pond.

Forlorn calls float by in the mist and then, soon after, an echoing cry comes back and they reverberate around the hills so they send a shiver from my head down to my boots. The rocks around my campsite seem black and the larger granite boulders are dark blue being heavy with the morning dampness. The whole scene appears prehistoric and untouched from its original state, as though day one was yesterday. On this day, however, these raged peaks are touched with misty clouds, and the gathering is like a swirling sea of carpet, and it seems I could walk from ridge to ridge on such a bridge. In a flight of fantasy, it is easy to behold His coming again in a cloud.

Time seems to have stopped its progression, as the scene before me is timeless, nothing has changed and it is comforting to see things as they were during my youth.

In these moments before dawn breaks when it seems the quietest, I hear a whisper of music falling on my ears, it's like the sound hummed by a celestial choir of angels; these sounds fill my soul, and even though I strain to capture their melodies they always just slip away from my grasp and roll over the hills and then down the slope to the valley below.

With these sounds and the surrounding, I grow quieter inside as I feel His presence hovering and brooding over the face of it all.

Now, early in the morning, God sees everything I see, and behold it is very good.

The further I trek, along this trail that winds upward, the more I feel that time has stood still; and it has become a place to commune with God one on one; and a place to work out fears and concerns uninterrupted. For me, this is my prayer closet, while away from home.

A wilderness can be something different for each of us, depending on circumstances. It could be miles and miles of desert sands or an uninhabited land, or perhaps a dense forest with smoky hills, or mountains. Some folks may be struggling with their own private wilderness on any corner of Main Street America, and they may be murmuring against God for their plight or demanding to have God rescue them from their wilderness. But sadly, they do not have a Moses to lead the way, toward a promised land. Their hunger for something beyond self might only be the temporary solution of a Big Mac and not the Manna from God. Those who are lost in their own forest dark, lack a compass to direct them out of their difficulties.

It is easy to recognize most individuals who are lost, for whatever reason, in a private wilderness. We just need to be alert to the signals they emit, in order to help our fellow men and women find the way to a richer, more satisfying life on planet earth.

Deep in the Heart of ME

There is a place without form.
Original, yet majestic and serene.
Thing's eternal is crystallized here.
Visions of day one prevails
and, I feel transported back in time
to those very first few
tick…tick…ticks.

There is a place untouched, unchanged.
It's primal and pristine.
Soaring granite peaks are covered
With a diadem of misty clouds,
Like swirling seas of serenity.
And it appears I could walk
From ridge to ridge.

There is a place, a timeless preserve,
It's like a fortress, or a keep.
Where cliffs and rocks
tall Pines and streams,
Moose, Bears, Deer and Fish
are the raw materials of?
existence to deal with.

There is a place, an empty waste.
It's a wilderness supreme.
In hazy shades of blue, grey and green.
A mystical peace touches my heart
and I sense His Spirit,
hovering and brooding
over the face of it all.

There is a place of perfect rest
where heaven came down.
Eerie calls echo round the hills,
and send a shiver from head to boot.
The music of it all fills my soul.
I strain to capture the melody;
but it slips away to the valley below.

Maine-ly Dreams

Lines of Pines and craggy heights.
with misty halos 'round each peak.
I'm watching eagles soaring high.
My dream begins this way.
But for now, it seems way out of reach.
It's for a distant time and place.
Ah, so many things I want to do.
I'll catch my dream someday.

I'll sail these seas to all points soon,
From north to south and east to west.
And all their wonders I will touch.
When I sail away someday.

Rocks and docks and quiet coves.
With sailboats bobbing to and fro.
While tethered to the wind.
My dream goes on this way.
But now I turn away and sigh.
I can't get with it even if I try.
Ah, so many seas to sail on by.
I'll weave my dream someday.

I'll sail these seas to all points soon.
From north to south and east to west

And, all their wonders I will touch
When I sail away someday.

Loons and dunes and gentle tides.
With a rainbow blazing 'cross the sky.
Funny how it all seems so real.
My dream plays out this way.
Well now I seem to be in sync.
I set a new course for that-a-way.
Ah, so many ports for me see.
My dream comes true this way.

I'm sailing this world to all points now.
From north to south and east to west.
And all their wonders I will touch.
Before winter comes my way.

For a Summer's Day Away

Summer seems so short a space.

Sweet lazy walks along the water's edge,

Turns our legs to blue, even in July.

Wild roses bend with the salty breeze.

I pick one just for you.

Wish Summer didn't pass so fast.

Boo hoo, hoo, hoo.

July

Summertime in Maine seems to pass in a blink. It's hardly enough time to enjoy the steady cooling breezes off the Atlantic, or savor those lazy walks along the shore. Even in July and August the chill of the water turns my legs blue.

From May to late December my chief satisfaction is to hike my way along this rocky coast; and then rest awhile among the rocks at the edge of the sea, with the morning newspaper and a container of hot coffee. I read a little, search the horizon for boats coming or going and listen to the ocean sounds while I wonder and dream a little.

The beauty of this scene is inspirational, and it causes me to tremble with shear enjoyment of His creation. But when the incoming tide crashes on the rocks below my feet and the spray soaks my newspaper, then I'm forced to retreat up the rocky face of the cliff to a higher perch; not too high, but just high enough not to get wet.

Even during the late fall to early winter, when the temperature falls and the atmosphere is heavy, it's bracing to dress warmer and enjoy the ruggedness of my surroundings. The changes that come to the harbor seem hour by hour. Every once-in-a-while a fog bank will roll in, and within moments I cannot see the newspaper held in front of me; and in a blink the folks sitting on the beach mysteriously vanished into the fog.

Another time while sailing out of the harbor for the open sea, a squadron of twenty-four or so cigar shaped racing sail boat, suddenly breaks out of fog bank; and leading them all is their colorful spinnakers, billowing taunt with air. It's a spectacular sight. At first, this awesome sight startled me, and then, just as quickly as they appeared, the rest of the boats swept past me at some 8 or 9 knots.

Now, as summer moves to fall the beach is nearly deserted with the exception of one or two dog walkers.

All that lingers on the sandy beach are charred driftwood and the ashes from clambakes past. The last remaining sea rose blooms, that surrounded the cove, seem tired and ready to sleep.

Trees and Sumac shrubs, along with the sea rose bushes are bare, having changed from their greens and pink blooms, to the red and gold of September and October. So now the landscape has changed its hue, being stripped of those vibrant colors.

The grey of the granite hillside is visible now that the trees are bare, only the pine trees offer a touch of green. The scene now brings a glimmer of what the original Maine was like.

Once the visitors to this village have left and returned to their homes in Montreal, Boston, or NYC or DC, things slow down to the pace of Maine. All the hustle and bustle of the summer and fall visitors from near and far, in campers and cars no longer clog the narrow shore line roads.

The towns and villages along the coast are much quieter. So, it is at this time of year when the real Maine comes out of hiding. The quietness that these changes bring is special.

Now, there is time to reflect on where you have been and where you are headed.

In early morn, just before dawn, the mist hangs heavy over the cove and it turns everything grey; and with the mist comes that feeling of solitude and it settles over this hamlet like a blanket until late morning when the sun finally breaks through.

The loft of the boat house is cold, and overnight the window panes were touched with frost. So, I need to rekindle the fireplace to take the chill off the place and then boil water for a pot of coffee. Clearing a patch of frost from the window I see a crust of ice has formed on the puddles of water in the pathway leading down to the town docks. When, as the sun peeks above the horizon, the cold night air rises over the warmer water of the cove to bring us one Maine's rarest and most beautiful eye treats called "Smoke of the Water".

The stillness of the pre-dawn quiet has been broken by the muffled voices and mechanical sounds brought by the Lobstermen, who live here. They are at the dock getting ready to work their lines of traps that have been soaking for 3 or 4 days throughout the harbor, so, it's time to haul in the catch. Christmas dinner will include a lobster or two for many families here in the cove.

The homes of year-round residents are nestled amongst the pine trees on the hillside.

Already some folks have festive lights and ornaments decorating the exterior of the houses; and in a few homes decorated Christmas trees stand at the window.

Below the line of houses the harbor waters are calm and the multi colored lights from above reflect a merry dance around the shore line. Smoke from the chimneys wafts up slowly, and lingers over the harbor. The aroma brought with the chimney smoke, adds to the smells of the sea, and for me it is a heady balm.

Snow has begun to fall and the wind is swirling the flakes around the cove and pushing the remaining leaves of fall into the nooks and crannies of the mews.

Tree boughs and roof tops are dusted by these first flakes and the smell of winter is stronger now. The temperature is hovering between 25- and 30-degrees F. So, I think there could be an accumulation of an inch or two before the day passes.

The Captain's Old Boat

Down east at York Harbor, every summer it seems,
We'd spend the evening down at the dock,
scrubbing and fixing, this tired old boat,
just so it will stay afloat,
for another summer sailing the coast.

As the sky turns ablaze of reds and golds;
And the tall pines now stand in relief.
We watch a gaff rigged schooner heading for home
that's just out of sight, 'round the bend below,
where it will dock for the last time today.

After the chores were done for the day,
The captain reads us stories of treasures and caves,
Of courage and faith, and of men who prevailed,
by land and sea or high in the sky.
It still gives me goose bumps to hear them anew.

The sounds of the night slip over the cove.
The squeak of leather, the slap of a line;
and an eerie hoot, hoot, hoot.
He reminds us again of this world's need:
For kids who are not too easily spooked.

"Life is wild and restless, he warns,
So, question who is Lord of your heart;
and give yourself to higher things".
We promise to aspire to these old truths,
As all things seem possible on his old boat.

Well now, the seasons slipped by one by one;
And we grew stronger and braver with time,
Especially when we were assured anew....
that love is always here,
on the captain's old boat.

A Song for the Way

This life with all its challenges.

Often leaves me wondering why.

But then I see a vision of a cross.

Atop a misty hill.

So, if I ask does God still care?

It's so easy to reply.

For I know He is always near to me.

and watching over things each day.

And often when I talk to Him,

I need to wipe away a tear

when down upon my knees,

as His glory is so great,

So, who am I to doubt Him

in what happens on the way?

For I, a lowly traveler.

saved only by His grace.

And, if you ask the way to Him,

He'll show you in His Word

The wonder of salvation

and the glorious life ahead.

So, when you know the way, the truth.

Just make a simple plea.

the gift of life is there for you.

as He has already planned your way.

Breaking the Barrier to God

We rocket through time and space,

nearing barrier speed

at the top of the waves;

but the higher I climb

the more I am slowed.

Moving across the heavens

caught up in the race, I'm losing control

of my ups and downs, and my systems fail.

I wonder what's wrong

and who's steering the ship.

Shock waves and turbulence

buffet my way.

I pray for a hand to stabilize the craft.

I know what is needed, I know what is right.

As suddenly, I break through and all is serene.

For a Glorious Autumn Day

Fall storms churn the sea so angrily.
See the hills and valley prepare to slumber.
Smokey shrouds linger over this sleepy hamlet.
I hunker down easy at Ye Olde Inn.
Chowda, Lobsta, Scrod ond Scallops.
Thanksgiving fills the soul.
Yum, yum, yum, yum.

October

There is something special about the season turning from Summer toward Autumn, isn't there?

The change in colors begins the transformation, and then there is the quieter feel and look to folks as they return to the normal work-a-day world. Life for younger members of a family is controlled by the school regime and parents by work and indoor social happenings. Churches begin programs that include prepping for Missionary outreach efforts and, of course, Christmas Concerts or plays, or other presentations.

Maybe later, closer to November, and perhaps more so in the northern reaches of the State, the first snowfall of the Winter will arrive, and with it will come that warm cozy feeling you get sitting near a crackling fireplace, along with the aroma of baked goods wafting throughout from the kitchen that turns trigger memories of yesteryear and other first snows of the season, and the world seems at ease again.

Solitude

Too often we fail to take full advantage of the downtime we gain from being in a place such as coastal Maine after all the summer visitors have returned to their home north and south of the State. But, it's hard to deny the feeling of solitude when alone sitting high up among the rocky coast, just above the Atlantic Ocean. This kind of solitude should not be confused with loneliness.

Solitude is present and it reinforces what it must have been like during creation when life, as we know it, was not present. Here, there is only the whisper from the wind rushing by my ears and the sound of the rustling of tree branches that stand just below.

Solitude is a special place where talents and creative thought can be nurtured; however, solitude for some is rarely found anymore. We think we must be productive or proactive at something all the time, like going somewhere or doing something, anything but being idle.

Now we see people everywhere with a cell phone at their ear 24/7. There's no downtime for anyone. The total spectrum of hearing and seeing is taken up with nonstop clutter. We now tend to think we can't just sit around reading or for that matter thinking about situations or perhaps relatives, friends or communicating with God. Some folks think that is just wasting time!

Solitude is elusive for many folks; but to have a time to think, to activate our creative Juices, is not a time waster; especially when we stop to wonder at it all we survey and then realize that only God and us have this ability for creative thought.

The kind of solitude I'm thinking about, however, is a time reserved for self-development or wonderment. It is, also, a time to absorb information, and increasing your depth of knowledge, particularly of what God has offered us in His Word, the Bible, which is our singular textbook for living and winning.

Solitude offers a time to freshen our impressions, to clarify plans, or to develop a new direction, thought or idea. It takes time to recognize the benefits solitude offers us and reap the benefits. It takes a real effort to get the thoughts we have in dealing with everyday living out of your mind and thereby concentrate on solutions, doesn't it?

Someone, somewhere once wrote: "I have yet to find the companion that was as companionable as solitude. I think it was Thoreau.

As I survey the majesty of my surroundings along this rock-bound Coast, I feel a sense of discovery and renewal. I should have placed a special marker here, as this is the place where I left my past life, buried forever, forgiven and forgotten, and where I readied myself to take that giant step of faith forward toward the rest of my life. This is also the place where I discovered how much of my life had been lived the wrong way, and it is here where I made a determination to turn things around.

So, in this solitude, my mind functions unfettered with concerns about what was, is, or will become. Instead, I am focused on the things that surrounded my life and as I sifted through the files stored in my mind over the years, I mentally made two stacks of these issues, one of which I labeled "Keepers" and the others I labeled "Dumpers", and as I worked my way through the files, the stack of dumpers grew and grew.

Now that I am left with only "Keepers", I have more time to do the things that I believe are important to my future development; and the opportunities that lie ahead cause me to become more and more excited about all the possibilities. I feel I am on the right track.

Before embarking on this new course, this phase two of my life, I searched for the things I felt were true possibilities for me going forward. After eliminating so much stuff, like places and people and things; I realized that what I discovered was a revelation. It's that supernatural spirit, virtually a supernatural consultant, I needed inside to lead the way forward.

Now, I have the steps in place to move upward and onward to the life I am now committed. I believe this life is there for everyone. It's that full, rich, bountiful,

satisfying and rewarding life just a few trembling steps ahead. Now, these steps to this new life are not so easy to take, but they are simple.

Often, the things, the influences, of outside pressures conspired against ones determination, and become great distractions. As I dealt with these imposters, that would distract from my objective, I concluded they were just this society's seduction, designed to keep me from the winning path I had set before me.

It was during one of my treks through this area, I discovered The Law of Dominate Thought which, for me, meant controlling what I allowed to be uppermost in my thoughts, or the dominant thoughts in my mind. This way of thinking became the root of my dealing with just about everything I encountered in everyday dealings with situations, people, and the Christian Walk.

I found that by working hard at controlling my thought processes and being consistent in my dealings with others I became what I repeatedly did…as a result, it became a habit, and I gained confidence. I became more reliable and trustworthy. In addition, communications became easier, more open, which spawned opportunities to contribute to others.

I kept reminding myself that the nature of this change in me was simplicity. Once I had the things in place, I learned to narrow my focus and purpose. As a result, I broadened into this new life and purpose, where I am totally free and in a partnership of control and direction.

Sometimes on our way.
We may have pain and a few sorrows.
But, if we are wise, we know there's
One we can turn to.
When we have a burden, that just overwhelms
and, it's hard to handle alone.
Just call on the father, to lend you a hand.
He's always near to carry you through.
Call on God, when trials come our way.
And He'll hear our plea. He will see us through.
Then, it won't be long 'til the sun breaks through
and, our world is bright again.
Call on God, when we're not strong.
And he'll give us strength to meet our need.
Then, it won't be long 'til our cares are gone
and we hear our song again.
Just swallow our pride
when we need help to just carry on.
We know he has the power to meet the needs
that we don't let show.
Then when your going is toughest,
seek out a friend whose burden is too much to bear,

and be that somebody they can turn to,
That's when our burdens will fade to light,
When life seems too heavy to bear.
He's close at hand so, just trust it to Him.
Call on Him... I know I can.
Just call on Him... Call on Him.

Sailing

The sun is low in the west
Clouds of gold streak the sky
Sailing home, sailing home.
It's a wonderful, wonderful place.
As my island comes into view
the sea is crashing on the shore.
Sailing home, Sailing home.
It's a wonderful, wonderful sight
Catch the wind on the tide.
Reef the sail as we glide.
Almost home, almost home.
It's a wonderful, wonderful life.
Swaying Palms frame the cove
in vibrant shades of green
Now I'm home, now I'm home.
It's a wonderful, wonderful gift.

For the First Snow of a Winter's Day

Winter blows in cold, dull and drear.
Buoy bells ring so differently now.
Tunes of gloria fill the air.
Warm glowing churches present timeless plays.
Children recite praises every which way
while smiling parents sigh in dismay.
Ho, ho, ho, ho.

December

Countdown To Christmas

It's starting...that great feeling is starting again...I'm feeling the excitement when I anticipate Christmas again.

It is very much like the feeling of anticipation when my daughters were born... can you imagine...pondering such great happenings during May, June, and April.

First, we will set up the Christmas Tree. Get all the decorations sorted... all the Figures of the Carolers...touch up the three wise men clad in ethnic costumes, for outdoors with a sign that reports: *Wise men still seek Him.*

Thanksgiving Day usually means a jump start to Christmas by watching Christmas Movies...beginning with Miracle on 34th St...and then most anything that has a Christmas tree in it...and all the Christmas music...WOW...what a time of year! If they asked me, I could write a book.

Recently I watched a "man in the street" reporter asking of passers-by the question, "What was Christmas all about?" Well, the answers were varied to say the least. The reporter showed only one in eight who answered, "Christmas is the annual celebration of the Birth of Jesus Christ."

Christmas to businesses is all about the big time Business of the Retail and Online purveyors of gifts for Christmas giving. However, the Business of God is quite different, even though there is a very unique gift involved; but it's offered free for the taking. The Business of God is not seasonal, it's ongoing day in and day out.

What it's all about

The Old Testament prophets did not know when their words would come to pass; they simply recorded what the Spirit of God showed them. So, when Isaiah wrote. *"Behold, a virgin shall be with child, and shall bring forth a son, and they shall call His name Emmanuel"* (Matt. 1:23 and Isaiah 7:14) he had no idea when this event would take place.

Emmanuel means *"God with us."* Jesus' presence on earth was the first step in reestablishing the intimacy man lost in the Garden of Eden. His life was God's personal expression of loving intent toward us. Today, we can rejoice in the incomparable blessing of living within the fulfillment of the promise the Lord gave the world through Isaiah thousands of years ago.

"I am with you always, even to the end of the age."
Matthew 28:20

God loves commemoration.

Throughout biblical history, we see Him marking significant events with a monument—or calling for an annual feast to memorialize a specific time when He showed His incredible saving power and love to His people.

Why is it important to keep such observances? Well, it's because God wants us to remember who He is and what He's done for us in a deeper way. He knows we need to experience a reality with both body and soul to truly understand it in its fullness.

At Christmas, believers have the opportunity to commemorate and celebrate a wonderful event unlike any other: when God put on flesh and came into the world to show us the way back to Him.

I shall remember the deeds of the Lord; surly I will remember Your wonders of old."

Psalm 77:11.

The Arrival

Jesus' birth came at a time when spiritual darkness covered the land. The people of Israel had all but forsaken the ways of the Lord. The temple had become a marketplace; sacrifices were offered for the sake of obligation and tradition rather than from an inner hunger to worship God. And hope for the coming Messiah was often a worldly desire for military salvation and the destruction of the Roman oppressors.

But Jesus came for a purpose that completely transcended those ways of thinking. Truly, He came to destroy the works of the enemy—that is, the enemy of our souls. He established His kingdom on earth by laying down His life as an offering of love and forgiveness—so that all men and women might have true abundant life.

"The people who walk in darkness will see a great light; those who live in a dark land, the light will shine on them."

Isaiah 9:2:

The Founder of Christendom

Who else has been preceded by hundreds of prophecies about His birth, life, and death?

Who else has been conceived in the most miraculous way possible?

Who else has merited a birth announcement from the hosts of heaven?

Who else would have inspired shepherds to leave behind their flocks to find Him?

No, Not One... He was not just another infant born of lowly status. He was, is, and always will be Jesus Christ, King of Kings and Lord of Lords.

The full message of Christmas is that eternal God came to earth as a man to save His own creations.

The message of Christmas doesn't end with the tiny baby wrapped in swaddling clothes and lying in a manger. That tiny baby came for a purpose: He came to die.

This tiny baby is the same person whose hands were nailed to the cross. His are the same hands that neatly folded His own burial wrappings and defeated sin and death so that He might give us eternal life. And this is the same person who reaches down to pick us up over and over again, throughout our often-difficult life.

"Oh, the depth of the riches both of the wisdom and knowledge of God! How unsearchable are his judgments, and his ways past finding out!"

Romans 11:33.

The Supreme Promise

Prophet after prophet foretold the Messiah's coming. Many of Israel's customs and feasts were shadows of the substance that would come with His appearing. Yet as one century after another went by, life seemed to go on as usual without the promised divine interruption. Were the words of God to His people only empty promises? Were all the prophets wrong? Was man destined to live in the chains of sin and bondage?

Then, on a day that began much like any other, that longed-for divine interruption came in the form of a baby who would change the destiny of humankind. For all those who were still waiting for Him, Jesus came quietly and without fanfare. But on the day of His birth, the world changed PROFOUNDLY. Nothing would ever be the same again.

"Arise, shine; for your light has come, and the glory of the Lord has risen upon you."

Isaiah 60:1.

Our Hope

One symbol of this coming redemption was the role of the *kinsman-redeemer*, a close family member who could choose to rescue a relative by paying his debts.

The fulfillment of Isaiah's prophecy is Jesus, who became our *kinsman-redeemer*; who became flesh and blood so that He might share in our humanity, thus becoming the Son of Man as well as Son of God. He walked with us, He identified with us so that He could pay our debts and show us the way back to our Creator. No one else could have delivered us from our sins and freed us from bondage.

"The spirit of the Lord God is upon me; Because the Lord hath anointed me to preach good tidings unto the meek; He hath sent me to bind up the broken-hearted".

Isaiah 61:1

Outgoing Love

Do you think our world is all that different from the time when Jesus was born? Just as in the times of Jesus, we have wars, social and political unrest, oppression, and fears, which were, and are, the realities of life. People of His time on earth were striving for the same things we long for today: peace, love, security and a sense of purpose. Jesus came to reveal Himself as the way for our heart to experience peace, contentment and love that lasts forever. If we live solely for societal satisfaction, we will find gratification is always temporary. The soul-satisfying, unconditional love of Jesus Christ came to present to us, is ours when we embrace Him and receive His freely-given gift. Jesus said unto him,

"I am the way, the truth and the life; no man cometh unto the father, but by me."

John 14:6

Altered Lives

The night Jesus was born; the shepherds became His first witnesses. Imagine how the news spread, from person to person. Bethlehem was full of travelers, and it would have been hard to ignore the shepherds wonder and excitement.

From His birth to His ascension, Jesus changes lives; and He is impacting lives to this day. Like the shepherds that first Christmas, we are His messengers when we share with others the great gift with those who are hurting or aimlessly searching for some sense to their life.

"And all things are of God, who hath reconciled us to himself by Jesus Christ, and hath given to us the ministry of reconciliation;

V 19...TO wit, that God was in Christ reconciling the world unto himself, not imputing their trespasses unto them; and hath committed unto us the word of reconciliation."

2 Corinthians 5:18-19.

The Gift

The gifts from God, I've lived to see.
Like mountain peaks touching western skies.
To desert winds and canyons deep.
I thank the Lord for sharing them with me.
The summer's glow over field of gold.
Forests aflame with colors bold
are not for me, just scenery.
Oh, thank you Lord. Oh, thank you Lord.
When winter blows o'er rolling hills,
and comes to rest on ocean shores.
From sea to sea, ah, such majesty.
I thank the Lord for sharing them with me.
For what He's given; His son the gift
We shouldn't take it too casually.
For all my days, in many ways
I'll thank the Lord. I'll thank the Lord.

The Star of Bethlehem

Suddenly before my eyes
Scenes of Christmastime arrive.
With them how my spirits rise,
The World seems all aglow.

Angels now appearing sing,
With Heavenly hosts praising Him.
Hosannas in the highest ring,
Above the Star of Bethlehem.

There in a lowly stable stall,
Lies God's Perfect Gift to all.
This Dayspring from on high
Comes to seek and save.

Behold, the Star of the East sends,
Radiant rays of hope for all mankind.
Darkness fades away to light.
His Star sets hearts a-flame.

Softly now comes Christmas morn,
And I awake to make my plea:
Write my name within that book.
His matchless gift brings life anew.

Mary's Song

Came the Angel Gabriel,
With a Heavenly Host appeared,
And a special Star aglow in the sky.
a special Star aglow in the sky.
Now the Heavenly Choir praises the Lord
And sings her song.

And Mary sits, lost in thought
While the haunting heavenly Aire,
That the Angels play so softly above
so softly above, so softly above.
All entranced she hears
That sweet serenade of long ago.

All the while her wonder grows
as the visions come and go.
Ah, what mystery alters her low estate?
Her calling awakes the midwinter night.

How can it be she is so blessed?
Laying Jesus on a soft bed.
Celestial bells ringing in time.
Oh, how they chime, and they ring, ding, ding.
Mary kept these things.
And pondered them in her heart.

Shepherds came unto Bethlehem
to see what had come to pass.

As the stable grew bright with dawns early glow
the stable grew bright with dawns early glow.
And, the Angel Gabriel having shared the news
Has drifted above.

But Mary still hears that sweet serenade of long, long ago.

It's Christmas Again

Softly, so softly, the first snow is falling.
O may, O may it stay for a while.
As winter arrives it's time to be trimming the tree and laughing.
It's Christmas again, and every eye is shining.

Is it really that long ago?
When we became one, to have and to hold?
Does the music of that eve still linger
or is it fading like a dream?

Come closer my dear and see the tree glowing.
Now, picture again that very first year,
When our hearts were soaring.

So fast, so fast the memories are flowing.
I hope, I hope they stay for a while.
It's Christmas again and carols are playing, and everyone is
singing
It's Christmas again, O, it's Christmas again.

Now that it's just we two alone
to dance beside this year's tree.
Is it still the joy of Christmas we share
or the joy of just being nearby?

Be closer my dear and see how it sparkles,
As we visit again our very first year
Beside the hearth still glowing

Away, away the seasons are passing
I wish, I wish they'd slow for awhile
Stay close my dear, and promise again, we will dance by the tree
Our very next year, When it's Christmas again.

A Spectacular Finish

Life is fantastic, isn't it?

We really need a special sense of humor to see the fun of it. With so many complexities being resolved by the simplest answers it amazes me to find our enlightened society, with so many intelligent and gifted people, fail to find the answers to their difficulties and continue to stagger through life as they compound one error with another.

It is difficult to shut out the noise from the rabble of this society for any length of time before a new more urgent demand raises its head, seeking instant gratification.

Just the day-to-day activities prohibit quietness and as a result it is more difficult to maintain our perspective on the things we establish as important. When we allow the rabble to occupy the mind, and, if we fail to dump it all into the permanent delete bin, we lose.

When we fail to make a commitment to excellence, in virtually any endeavor, it doesn't matter if the instructor has the wisdom of Solomon, and/or the eloquence of Apollos, the teaching will be ineffective.

Sometimes, when we have been working under pressure, for a sustained period of time, meaning can slip away from our endeavors, and the substitutes we seek ultimately fail to satisfy those desires we have way down deep inside.

So, once, when I was so affected, and not reaching my goals in a timely way, I decided to put in place a new series of steps to see the progress I had envisioned. Being an upwardly mobile worker I decided to build a ladder to success: I limited the rungs in the ladder to just four, namely: Desire, Dedication, Determination, and Discipline.

This system worked pretty well, but I was still left with that itch deep down inside where you know something is missing.

So, I began the search for that something to connect with, to merge all the parts of my system together and get the most out of: Mind, Soul, and Physical Well Being.

You know to purify gold it is necessary to heat it to an extremely high temperature until it turns molten. Once gold is molten, all the impurities rise to the surface. It is then that these impurities can be raked-off until not the slightest speck is left in the molten gold. It is then, and only then, a bar of gold is stamped 6666 pure. The purest you can get!

This is the level of purification I wanted as my life goal. I determined that if I aspire to a set of Principals or Standards to live by; and set them in place unreservedly in my heart of hearts, (That's the place only you and God knows.) and if attained, you will have more success and deep-down satisfaction than you ever dreamt possible.

The thing is, only you can set the Principals or Standards by which you want to live, and what you stand for. If you set frivolous Principals or Standards your life will be equally frivolous.

However, if you choose wisely and set High Standards and Noble Principals that require courage and honesty to maintain, then your life will be equally Glorious and Noble; and you will have made a positive contribution to society.

The best thing, after all, is outgoing love that you offer to friend and foe alike. It's the one thing that will always come back to you tenfold. Outgoing Love will turn your world around.

God must love the spectacular. He splashes His paints across the evening sky and it creates the beauty we frame.

God makes a sea out of glass, to reflect the bold and breathless colors of His throne. He builds His streets out of gold instead of concrete. He calls upon the wind, with a touch of lightning and the crashing cymbals for His thunder-to be His overture. He has more galaxies than any computer, even goggle number, can count. I wonder if He leaves one empty just for fireworks-for His pleasure and ours.

So, however God did it, it was spectacular for sure!

Now, ask yourself, "Are we any-the-less spectacular, when we turn our lives over to God"?

Each of us has a choice as to how our story ends. It can end with us slumped in the wreckage of wasted lives, or it can end in the most spectacular rescue of all time.

His offer is on the table! No need to negotiate, it's a one-word response: No or Yes.

The life of a trusting Christian is constantly spectacular. It is a succession of miracles.

Take time to ponder, during this season, about people, places, events, and His Word.

"Now, the Lord of peace himself gave you peace always by all means."

2 Thessalonians 3: 16.

An Old-Fashioned Idea

I have been inspired by the outstanding character of our daughter, which she exhibited as she dealt with her serious health issues over the past several years.

I am, therefore, obliged to undertake an adventure of my own to be an example worthy of her courage and tenacity.

Not only is it a Christian duty, our responsibility, but our deeper raison d'etres, and an unwritten obligation to act honorably, generously, respectably, and responsibly toward one another, and to fulfill our Christian and social responsibilities.

This old-fashioned idea is called Noblesse Oblige. Which many centuries ago was applied primarily to wealthy aristocrats, to be of service to those of the population not so blessed with wealth or opportunities.

It seems to me these characteristics have been watered down, or are more than somewhat lacking in much of today's society. The chief cause, for the demise of this grand old social norm, is a falling away from God at virtually every level of society.

So, my thoughts of late have been centered on the need to encourage Men and Women of the Faith to get back to basics, by developing programs, or a curriculum to raise the profile and intelligence quantum, and pass it on to the young members of our families.

Christianity is the conscience of the country, so it is important to set high standards and live by them, for the good of the Country and this Cause.

This program should foster Creativity, and include a sense of Belonging, Independence, Mastery and Generosity, Parental Respect, and God's Holy Word, in order to nullify the negative influences, and the dumbing down of this society.

We cannot trust Educators or the education system as it is currently formatted to do this. We cannot rely on the Government or Society to generate the correct impact, because those institutions have failed.

In order to counteract this current trend, we need a revolution of sorts, by Christian Men and Women, to impact the younger generation with the right stuff, such as character-building principles that will, in time, bring a more satisfying lifestyle to America's youth and subsequently build a generation of greatness, like no other.

www.ingramcontent.com/pod-product-compliance
Lightning Source LLC
Chambersburg PA
CBHW061342120726
48001CB00002B/986